50 Grill and Chill Recipes for Home

By: Kelly Johnson

Table of Contents

- Classic Cheeseburgers
- Grilled Chicken Skewers
- BBQ Ribs
- Vegetable Kabobs
- Grilled Salmon
- Stuffed Peppers on the Grill
- Grilled Corn on the Cob
- Pineapple Teriyaki Chicken
- Beef Tacos with Grilled Vegetables
- Lemon Herb Grilled Shrimp
- Zucchini and Squash Fritters
- Spicy Grilled Sausages
- Caprese Salad Skewers
- BBQ Pulled Pork Sandwiches
- Grilled Eggplant Slices
- Lime Cilantro Grilled Chicken
- Stuffed Portobello Mushrooms
- Grilled Flatbreads
- Honey Balsamic Glazed Carrots
- Grilled Caesar Salad
- Chipotle Chicken Tacos
- Savory Grilled Lamb Chops
- Grilled Shrimp Tacos
- Balsamic Grilled Vegetables
- Grilled Peach Salad
- Garlic Butter Grilled Corn
- Smoky BBQ Chicken Wings
- Cilantro Lime Rice Bowl
- Grilled Fish Tacos
- Honey Mustard Chicken Thighs
- Spicy Grilled Cauliflower Steaks
- S'mores on the Grill

- Mediterranean Grilled Chicken
- Grilled Asparagus with Parmesan
- Barbecue Beef Brisket
- Grilled Stuffed Zucchini Boats
- Buffalo Grilled Chicken Bites
- Grilled Watermelon Salad
- Teriyaki Beef Skewers
- Grilled Shrimp and Grits
- Sausage and Pepper Hoagies
- Grilled Chicken Fajitas
- Corn and Avocado Salsa
- Grilled Apple Crisp
- Sesame Ginger Grilled Tofu
- Mango Salsa for Grilled Fish
- Grilled Potatoes with Rosemary
- Marinated Grilled Pork Chops
- Coconut Lime Grilled Chicken
- Grilled Chocolate Banana Boats

Classic Cheeseburgers

Ingredients

- 1 lb ground beef
- 1 teaspoon garlic powder
- 1 teaspoon onion powder
- Salt and pepper to taste
- 4 slices of cheese (cheddar, American, or your choice)
- 4 hamburger buns
- Lettuce, tomato, onion, and condiments for serving

Instructions

1. **Preheat Grill:** Preheat your grill to medium-high heat.
2. **Mix Ingredients:** In a bowl, combine ground beef, garlic powder, onion powder, salt, and pepper. Form into 4 patties.
3. **Grill Patties:** Grill patties for about 4-5 minutes per side, or until desired doneness. Add cheese during the last minute to melt.
4. **Assemble Burgers:** Place patties on buns and top with lettuce, tomato, onion, and condiments.
5. **Serve:** Enjoy immediately!

Grilled Chicken Skewers

Ingredients

- 1 lb chicken breast, cubed
- 2 tablespoons olive oil
- 2 tablespoons soy sauce
- 1 tablespoon honey
- 1 teaspoon garlic powder
- Assorted vegetables (bell peppers, onions, zucchini)

Instructions

1. **Marinate Chicken:** In a bowl, mix olive oil, soy sauce, honey, garlic powder, and cubed chicken. Marinate for at least 30 minutes.
2. **Prepare Skewers:** Thread marinated chicken and vegetables onto skewers.
3. **Preheat Grill:** Preheat the grill to medium heat.
4. **Grill Skewers:** Grill skewers for about 10-12 minutes, turning occasionally, until chicken is cooked through.
5. **Serve:** Enjoy hot!

BBQ Ribs

Ingredients

- 2 lbs baby back ribs
- 1 cup BBQ sauce
- Salt and pepper to taste
- Optional: dry rub spices (paprika, garlic powder, brown sugar)

Instructions

1. **Preheat Grill:** Preheat your grill to medium heat.
2. **Prepare Ribs:** Season ribs with salt, pepper, and any dry rub spices if using.
3. **Grill Ribs:** Place ribs on the grill, meat side down, and cook for about 1 hour, flipping occasionally.
4. **Add BBQ Sauce:** Brush BBQ sauce on ribs during the last 15 minutes of grilling.
5. **Serve:** Enjoy with extra BBQ sauce on the side!

Vegetable Kabobs

Ingredients

- 2 cups assorted vegetables (bell peppers, mushrooms, zucchini, cherry tomatoes)
- 2 tablespoons olive oil
- 1 teaspoon Italian seasoning
- Salt and pepper to taste

Instructions

1. **Preheat Grill:** Preheat your grill to medium heat.
2. **Prepare Vegetables:** In a bowl, toss vegetables with olive oil, Italian seasoning, salt, and pepper.
3. **Assemble Kabobs:** Thread vegetables onto skewers.
4. **Grill Kabobs:** Grill for about 10-15 minutes, turning occasionally, until tender and slightly charred.
5. **Serve:** Enjoy warm!

Grilled Salmon

Ingredients

- 4 salmon fillets
- 2 tablespoons olive oil
- 1 tablespoon lemon juice
- Salt and pepper to taste
- Lemon wedges for serving

Instructions

1. **Preheat Grill:** Preheat your grill to medium-high heat.
2. **Season Salmon:** Brush salmon fillets with olive oil, lemon juice, salt, and pepper.
3. **Grill Salmon:** Place salmon skin-side down on the grill. Grill for about 5-7 minutes per side, or until cooked through.
4. **Serve:** Serve with lemon wedges. Enjoy!

Stuffed Peppers on the Grill

Ingredients

- 4 bell peppers, halved and seeded
- 1 lb ground beef or turkey
- 1 cup cooked rice
- 1 cup marinara sauce
- 1 cup shredded cheese
- Salt and pepper to taste
  ### Instructions
1. **Preheat Grill:** Preheat your grill to medium heat.
2. **Cook Filling:** In a skillet, cook ground meat until browned. Mix in rice, marinara sauce, salt, and pepper.
3. **Stuff Peppers:** Fill each pepper half with the meat mixture and top with cheese.
4. **Grill Peppers:** Place stuffed peppers on the grill and cook for about 20-25 minutes, or until peppers are tender.
5. **Serve:** Enjoy warm!

Grilled Corn on the Cob

Ingredients

- 4 ears of corn, husked
- 2 tablespoons butter
- Salt to taste

Instructions

1. **Preheat Grill:** Preheat your grill to medium heat.
2. **Prepare Corn:** Soak corn in water for 10-15 minutes (optional) to keep it moist.
3. **Grill Corn:** Place corn on the grill and cook for about 10-15 minutes, turning occasionally, until tender and charred.
4. **Serve:** Brush with butter and sprinkle with salt before enjoying!

Pineapple Teriyaki Chicken

Ingredients

- 1 lb chicken thighs or breasts
- ½ cup teriyaki sauce
- 1 cup fresh pineapple chunks
- 2 tablespoons sesame seeds (optional)

Instructions

1. **Marinate Chicken:** In a bowl, combine chicken and teriyaki sauce. Marinate for at least 30 minutes.
2. **Preheat Grill:** Preheat your grill to medium-high heat.
3. **Grill Chicken:** Grill chicken for about 6-8 minutes per side, or until cooked through.
4. **Add Pineapple:** During the last few minutes, add pineapple chunks to the grill until caramelized.
5. **Serve:** Sprinkle with sesame seeds if desired and enjoy!

Beef Tacos with Grilled Vegetables

Ingredients

- 1 lb ground beef
- 1 packet taco seasoning
- 8 small corn or flour tortillas
- 1 bell pepper, sliced
- 1 zucchini, sliced
- 1 onion, sliced
- Olive oil for grilling
- Toppings: salsa, cheese, avocado, cilantro
  Instructions
1. **Cook Beef:** In a skillet, cook ground beef over medium heat until browned. Add taco seasoning and follow package instructions.
2. **Grill Vegetables:** Preheat grill and toss sliced vegetables in olive oil. Grill for 5-7 minutes until tender.
3. **Warm Tortillas:** Warm tortillas on the grill for about 30 seconds per side.
4. **Assemble Tacos:** Fill tortillas with beef and grilled vegetables. Add desired toppings.
5. **Serve:** Enjoy immediately!

Lemon Herb Grilled Shrimp

Ingredients

- 1 lb large shrimp, peeled and deveined
- 2 tablespoons olive oil
- 2 tablespoons lemon juice
- 1 teaspoon garlic powder
- 1 teaspoon dried oregano
- Salt and pepper to taste

Instructions

1. **Marinate Shrimp:** In a bowl, combine shrimp, olive oil, lemon juice, garlic powder, oregano, salt, and pepper. Marinate for 15-30 minutes.
2. **Preheat Grill:** Preheat your grill to medium-high heat.
3. **Skewer Shrimp:** Thread shrimp onto skewers.
4. **Grill Shrimp:** Grill for 2-3 minutes per side until shrimp are opaque and cooked through.
5. **Serve:** Enjoy warm!

Zucchini and Squash Fritters

Ingredients

- 2 cups grated zucchini
- 2 cups grated yellow squash
- 1 cup breadcrumbs
- 2 large eggs
- ½ cup grated Parmesan cheese
- Salt and pepper to taste
- Olive oil for frying

Instructions

1. **Prepare Zucchini:** Squeeze grated zucchini and squash to remove excess moisture.
2. **Mix Ingredients:** In a bowl, combine zucchini, squash, breadcrumbs, eggs, Parmesan, salt, and pepper.
3. **Form Fritters:** Heat olive oil in a skillet over medium heat. Form the mixture into patties and cook for 3-4 minutes on each side until golden brown.
4. **Serve:** Enjoy warm with your favorite dipping sauce!

Spicy Grilled Sausages

Ingredients

- 4 spicy sausages (chorizo, Italian, or your choice)
- 1 tablespoon olive oil
- 1 bell pepper, sliced
- 1 onion, sliced
- Buns for serving (optional)

Instructions

1. **Preheat Grill:** Preheat your grill to medium heat.
2. **Prepare Vegetables:** Toss sliced peppers and onions in olive oil.
3. **Grill Sausages:** Grill sausages for about 12-15 minutes, turning occasionally until cooked through.
4. **Grill Vegetables:** Grill peppers and onions for about 5-7 minutes until tender.
5. **Serve:** Serve sausages in buns with grilled vegetables on the side or on top.

Caprese Salad Skewers

Ingredients

- 1 pint cherry tomatoes
- 8 oz fresh mozzarella balls
- Fresh basil leaves
- Balsamic glaze for drizzling
- Salt and pepper to taste

Instructions

1. **Assemble Skewers:** On small skewers or toothpicks, thread a cherry tomato, a basil leaf, and a mozzarella ball. Repeat until skewers are filled.
2. **Drizzle:** Arrange on a platter and drizzle with balsamic glaze.
3. **Season:** Sprinkle with salt and pepper.
4. **Serve:** Enjoy as a fresh appetizer!

BBQ Pulled Pork Sandwiches

Ingredients

- 2 lbs pork shoulder
- 1 cup BBQ sauce
- 1 onion, sliced
- 4 hamburger buns
- Coleslaw for topping (optional)

Instructions

1. **Cook Pork:** In a slow cooker, place pork shoulder and onion. Cover with BBQ sauce. Cook on low for 8 hours or until tender.
2. **Shred Pork:** Remove pork, shred with forks, and return to the slow cooker to mix with the sauce.
3. **Serve:** Spoon pulled pork onto buns and top with coleslaw if desired. Enjoy!

Grilled Eggplant Slices

Ingredients

- 1 large eggplant, sliced into ½-inch rounds
- 3 tablespoons olive oil
- 1 teaspoon garlic powder
- Salt and pepper to taste

Instructions

1. **Preheat Grill:** Preheat your grill to medium heat.
2. **Prepare Eggplant:** Brush eggplant slices with olive oil and season with garlic powder, salt, and pepper.
3. **Grill Eggplant:** Grill slices for about 4-5 minutes per side until tender and grill marks appear.
4. **Serve:** Enjoy warm as a side dish or appetizer!

Lime Cilantro Grilled Chicken

Ingredients

- 1 lb chicken breasts
- 2 tablespoons olive oil
- 2 tablespoons lime juice
- 1 teaspoon cumin
- ¼ cup chopped fresh cilantro
- Salt and pepper to taste

Instructions

1. **Marinate Chicken:** In a bowl, mix olive oil, lime juice, cumin, cilantro, salt, and pepper. Add chicken and marinate for at least 30 minutes.
2. **Preheat Grill:** Preheat your grill to medium-high heat.
3. **Grill Chicken:** Grill chicken for about 6-7 minutes per side, or until cooked through.
4. **Serve:** Enjoy hot, garnished with extra cilantro if desired!

Stuffed Portobello Mushrooms

Ingredients

- 4 large portobello mushrooms
- 1 cup cooked quinoa
- 1 cup diced bell peppers
- ½ cup diced onion
- 1 cup shredded mozzarella cheese
- 2 tablespoons olive oil
- Salt and pepper to taste

Instructions

1. **Preheat Grill:** Preheat your grill to medium heat.
2. **Prepare Mushrooms:** Remove stems from portobello mushrooms and brush with olive oil. Season with salt and pepper.
3. **Mix Filling:** In a bowl, combine cooked quinoa, bell peppers, onion, and half of the mozzarella.
4. **Stuff Mushrooms:** Fill each mushroom cap with the quinoa mixture and top with remaining mozzarella.
5. **Grill Mushrooms:** Place on the grill and cook for 10-12 minutes, or until mushrooms are tender and cheese is melted.
6. **Serve:** Enjoy warm!

Grilled Flatbreads

Ingredients

- 2 cups all-purpose flour
- 1 teaspoon baking powder
- ½ teaspoon salt
- ¾ cup water
- 2 tablespoons olive oil

Instructions

1. **Mix Dough:** In a bowl, combine flour, baking powder, and salt. Gradually add water and olive oil, mixing until a dough forms.
2. **Knead Dough:** Knead on a floured surface for about 5 minutes until smooth.
3. **Shape Flatbreads:** Divide dough into 4 pieces and roll each into a thin circle.
4. **Preheat Grill:** Preheat your grill to medium-high heat.
5. **Grill Flatbreads:** Grill each flatbread for about 2-3 minutes per side, until lightly charred and cooked through.
6. **Serve:** Enjoy warm, topped with your favorite ingredients!

Honey Balsamic Glazed Carrots

Ingredients

- 1 lb baby carrots
- 2 tablespoons honey
- 2 tablespoons balsamic vinegar
- 1 tablespoon olive oil
- Salt and pepper to taste

Instructions

1. **Preheat Grill:** Preheat your grill to medium heat.
2. **Mix Glaze:** In a bowl, combine honey, balsamic vinegar, olive oil, salt, and pepper.
3. **Coat Carrots:** Toss baby carrots in the glaze until well coated.
4. **Grill Carrots:** Place carrots on the grill in a grill basket or foil pouch and cook for about 15-20 minutes, tossing occasionally, until tender.
5. **Serve:** Enjoy warm as a side dish!

Grilled Caesar Salad

Ingredients

- 1 head romaine lettuce, halved lengthwise
- 2 tablespoons olive oil
- Salt and pepper to taste
- ½ cup Caesar dressing
- Grated Parmesan cheese for serving
- Croutons for topping

Instructions

1. **Preheat Grill:** Preheat your grill to medium heat.
2. **Prepare Lettuce:** Brush cut sides of romaine with olive oil and season with salt and pepper.
3. **Grill Lettuce:** Grill romaine for about 2-3 minutes until lightly charred.
4. **Assemble Salad:** Drizzle with Caesar dressing, top with Parmesan cheese and croutons.
5. **Serve:** Enjoy warm!

Chipotle Chicken Tacos

Ingredients

- 1 lb chicken thighs, boneless and skinless
- 2 tablespoons chipotle sauce
- 8 small corn or flour tortillas
- Toppings: avocado, cilantro, lime wedges

Instructions

1. **Marinate Chicken:** In a bowl, mix chicken with chipotle sauce and marinate for at least 30 minutes.
2. **Preheat Grill:** Preheat your grill to medium-high heat.
3. **Grill Chicken:** Grill chicken for about 5-7 minutes per side, or until cooked through.
4. **Warm Tortillas:** Warm tortillas on the grill for about 30 seconds per side.
5. **Assemble Tacos:** Slice chicken and fill tortillas. Add toppings as desired.
6. **Serve:** Enjoy immediately!

Savory Grilled Lamb Chops

Ingredients

- 1 lb lamb chops
- 2 tablespoons olive oil
- 2 cloves garlic, minced
- 1 tablespoon fresh rosemary, chopped
- Salt and pepper to taste
   Instructions
1. **Marinate Lamb:** In a bowl, combine olive oil, garlic, rosemary, salt, and pepper. Coat lamb chops in the mixture and marinate for at least 30 minutes.
2. **Preheat Grill:** Preheat your grill to medium-high heat.
3. **Grill Lamb:** Grill lamb chops for about 4-5 minutes per side, or until desired doneness.
4. **Serve:** Enjoy warm!

Grilled Shrimp Tacos

Ingredients

- 1 lb shrimp, peeled and deveined
- 2 tablespoons olive oil
- 1 tablespoon lime juice
- 1 teaspoon cumin
- 8 small corn or flour tortillas
- Toppings: cabbage slaw, avocado, salsa

Instructions

1. **Marinate Shrimp:** In a bowl, combine shrimp, olive oil, lime juice, cumin, salt, and pepper. Marinate for 15-30 minutes.
2. **Preheat Grill:** Preheat your grill to medium-high heat.
3. **Grill Shrimp:** Grill shrimp for about 2-3 minutes per side until opaque and cooked through.
4. **Warm Tortillas:** Warm tortillas on the grill for about 30 seconds per side.
5. **Assemble Tacos:** Fill tortillas with grilled shrimp and toppings as desired.
6. **Serve:** Enjoy immediately!

Balsamic Grilled Vegetables

Ingredients

- 2 cups assorted vegetables (bell peppers, zucchini, mushrooms, red onion)
- 3 tablespoons balsamic vinegar
- 2 tablespoons olive oil
- Salt and pepper to taste

Instructions

1. **Preheat Grill:** Preheat your grill to medium heat.
2. **Prepare Vegetables:** In a bowl, toss vegetables with balsamic vinegar, olive oil, salt, and pepper.
3. **Grill Vegetables:** Place vegetables on the grill and cook for about 10-15 minutes, turning occasionally, until tender and charred.
4. **Serve:** Enjoy warm as a side dish!

Grilled Peach Salad

Ingredients

- 2 ripe peaches, halved and pitted
- 4 cups mixed greens
- ½ cup crumbled feta cheese
- ¼ cup walnuts, toasted
- 3 tablespoons olive oil
- 2 tablespoons balsamic vinegar
- Salt and pepper to taste

Instructions

1. **Preheat Grill:** Preheat your grill to medium heat.
2. **Grill Peaches:** Brush peach halves with olive oil and grill cut-side down for 3-4 minutes until caramelized.
3. **Assemble Salad:** In a large bowl, combine mixed greens, grilled peaches, feta cheese, and walnuts.
4. **Dress Salad:** In a small bowl, whisk together olive oil, balsamic vinegar, salt, and pepper. Drizzle over salad.
5. **Serve:** Enjoy immediately!

Garlic Butter Grilled Corn

Ingredients

- 4 ears of corn, husked
- ½ cup unsalted butter, melted
- 3 cloves garlic, minced
- Salt and pepper to taste
- Fresh parsley for garnish

Instructions

1. **Preheat Grill:** Preheat your grill to medium-high heat.
2. **Prepare Butter:** In a bowl, mix melted butter with minced garlic, salt, and pepper.
3. **Grill Corn:** Brush corn with garlic butter and grill for 10-15 minutes, turning occasionally, until tender and charred.
4. **Garnish:** Sprinkle with fresh parsley before serving.
5. **Serve:** Enjoy warm!

Smoky BBQ Chicken Wings

Ingredients

- 2 lbs chicken wings
- 1 cup BBQ sauce
- 1 teaspoon smoked paprika
- Salt and pepper to taste

Instructions

1. **Preheat Grill:** Preheat your grill to medium heat.
2. **Season Wings:** In a bowl, toss wings with smoked paprika, salt, and pepper.
3. **Grill Wings:** Grill wings for 20-25 minutes, turning occasionally, until cooked through and crispy.
4. **Add Sauce:** Brush wings with BBQ sauce during the last 5 minutes of grilling.
5. **Serve:** Enjoy with extra BBQ sauce on the side!

Cilantro Lime Rice Bowl

Ingredients

- 2 cups cooked rice
- ¼ cup fresh cilantro, chopped
- 2 tablespoons lime juice
- 1 teaspoon lime zest
- Salt to taste
- Optional toppings: black beans, corn, avocado
  ### Instructions
1. **Mix Rice:** In a bowl, combine cooked rice, cilantro, lime juice, lime zest, and salt.
2. **Stir:** Mix well until evenly combined.
3. **Serve:** Top with black beans, corn, and avocado if desired. Enjoy!

Grilled Fish Tacos

Ingredients

- 1 lb white fish (such as tilapia or mahi-mahi)
- 2 tablespoons olive oil
- 1 tablespoon lime juice
- Salt and pepper to taste
- 8 small corn or flour tortillas
- Toppings: cabbage slaw, avocado, salsa

Instructions

1. **Preheat Grill:** Preheat your grill to medium-high heat.
2. **Prepare Fish:** Brush fish with olive oil, lime juice, salt, and pepper.
3. **Grill Fish:** Grill fish for about 3-4 minutes per side, or until cooked through and flaky.
4. **Warm Tortillas:** Warm tortillas on the grill for about 30 seconds per side.
5. **Assemble Tacos:** Flake fish and fill tortillas. Add toppings as desired.
6. **Serve:** Enjoy immediately!

Honey Mustard Chicken Thighs

Ingredients

- 1.5 lbs chicken thighs, boneless and skinless
- ¼ cup honey
- ¼ cup Dijon mustard
- 2 tablespoons olive oil
- Salt and pepper to taste

Instructions

1. **Marinate Chicken:** In a bowl, whisk together honey, mustard, olive oil, salt, and pepper. Coat chicken thighs in the mixture and marinate for at least 30 minutes.
2. **Preheat Grill:** Preheat your grill to medium heat.
3. **Grill Chicken:** Grill chicken thighs for about 6-7 minutes per side, or until cooked through.
4. **Serve:** Enjoy warm!

Spicy Grilled Cauliflower Steaks

Ingredients

- 1 large head of cauliflower
- 3 tablespoons olive oil
- 1 teaspoon smoked paprika
- ½ teaspoon cayenne pepper
- Salt and pepper to taste

Instructions

1. **Preheat Grill:** Preheat your grill to medium-high heat.
2. **Prepare Cauliflower:** Slice cauliflower into thick steaks. Brush both sides with olive oil and season with paprika, cayenne, salt, and pepper.
3. **Grill Cauliflower:** Grill steaks for about 5-7 minutes per side until tender and charred.
4. **Serve:** Enjoy warm as a side or main dish!

S'mores on the Grill

Ingredients

- 8 graham crackers
- 4 chocolate bars
- 16 marshmallows

Instructions

1. **Preheat Grill:** Preheat your grill to medium heat.
2. **Assemble S'mores:** On half of the graham crackers, place a piece of chocolate and a marshmallow. Top with another graham cracker.
3. **Grill S'mores:** Place assembled s'mores on the grill for about 2-3 minutes, until the marshmallows are gooey and the chocolate is melted.
4. **Serve:** Enjoy warm and melty!

Mediterranean Grilled Chicken

Ingredients

- 4 chicken breasts
- ¼ cup olive oil
- 2 tablespoons lemon juice
- 2 teaspoons dried oregano
- 2 teaspoons garlic powder
- Salt and pepper to taste
  Instructions
1. **Marinate Chicken:** In a bowl, whisk together olive oil, lemon juice, oregano, garlic powder, salt, and pepper. Coat chicken breasts in the marinade and let sit for at least 30 minutes.
2. **Preheat Grill:** Preheat your grill to medium-high heat.
3. **Grill Chicken:** Grill chicken for about 6-7 minutes per side, or until cooked through.
4. **Serve:** Enjoy warm with your favorite sides!

Grilled Asparagus with Parmesan

Ingredients

- 1 lb asparagus, trimmed
- 2 tablespoons olive oil
- Salt and pepper to taste
- ½ cup grated Parmesan cheese

Instructions

1. **Preheat Grill:** Preheat your grill to medium-high heat.
2. **Prepare Asparagus:** Toss asparagus with olive oil, salt, and pepper.
3. **Grill Asparagus:** Grill for about 5-7 minutes, turning occasionally, until tender and slightly charred.
4. **Add Parmesan:** Sprinkle with Parmesan cheese just before serving.
5. **Serve:** Enjoy warm!

Barbecue Beef Brisket

Ingredients

- 3 lbs beef brisket
- 1 cup BBQ sauce
- 2 tablespoons brown sugar
- 1 tablespoon smoked paprika
- Salt and pepper to taste

Instructions

1. **Preheat Grill:** Preheat your grill for indirect cooking (one side on medium heat).
2. **Season Brisket:** Rub brisket with brown sugar, smoked paprika, salt, and pepper.
3. **Cook Brisket:** Place brisket on the cooler side of the grill and cook for 3-4 hours, basting with BBQ sauce every hour.
4. **Rest and Slice:** Let rest for 30 minutes before slicing.
5. **Serve:** Enjoy with additional BBQ sauce!

Grilled Stuffed Zucchini Boats

Ingredients

- 4 medium zucchinis, halved and seeded
- 1 cup cooked quinoa
- 1 cup diced tomatoes
- 1 cup shredded mozzarella cheese
- 2 tablespoons olive oil
- Salt and pepper to taste

Instructions

1. **Preheat Grill:** Preheat your grill to medium heat.
2. **Prepare Zucchini:** Brush zucchini halves with olive oil and season with salt and pepper.
3. **Mix Filling:** In a bowl, combine cooked quinoa, diced tomatoes, and half of the mozzarella.
4. **Stuff Zucchini:** Fill each zucchini half with the quinoa mixture and top with remaining mozzarella.
5. **Grill Zucchini:** Place on the grill and cook for about 15-20 minutes until tender and cheese is melted.
6. **Serve:** Enjoy warm!

Buffalo Grilled Chicken Bites

Ingredients

- 1 lb chicken breast, cut into bite-sized pieces
- ¼ cup buffalo sauce
- 2 tablespoons olive oil
- Salt and pepper to taste

Instructions

1. **Preheat Grill:** Preheat your grill to medium-high heat.
2. **Marinate Chicken:** In a bowl, toss chicken pieces with buffalo sauce, olive oil, salt, and pepper.
3. **Skewer Chicken:** Thread chicken onto skewers.
4. **Grill Chicken:** Grill for about 8-10 minutes, turning occasionally, until cooked through.
5. **Serve:** Enjoy with ranch or blue cheese dressing!

Grilled Watermelon Salad

Ingredients

- 4 cups watermelon, cut into cubes
- 1 tablespoon olive oil
- ¼ cup feta cheese, crumbled
- ¼ cup fresh mint, chopped
- Balsamic glaze for drizzling
  Instructions
1. **Preheat Grill:** Preheat your grill to medium heat.
2. **Grill Watermelon:** Toss watermelon cubes with olive oil and grill for about 2-3 minutes until grill marks appear.
3. **Assemble Salad:** In a bowl, combine grilled watermelon, feta cheese, and mint.
4. **Drizzle:** Drizzle with balsamic glaze before serving.
5. **Serve:** Enjoy chilled or at room temperature!

Teriyaki Beef Skewers

Ingredients

- 1 lb beef sirloin, cut into cubes
- ½ cup teriyaki sauce
- 2 tablespoons sesame oil
- 1 bell pepper, cut into squares
- 1 onion, cut into squares

Instructions

1. **Marinate Beef:** In a bowl, combine beef, teriyaki sauce, and sesame oil. Marinate for at least 30 minutes.
2. **Preheat Grill:** Preheat your grill to medium-high heat.
3. **Skewer Ingredients:** Thread beef, bell pepper, and onion onto skewers.
4. **Grill Skewers:** Grill for about 8-10 minutes, turning occasionally, until beef is cooked to your liking.
5. **Serve:** Enjoy with additional teriyaki sauce if desired!

Grilled Shrimp and Grits

Ingredients

- 1 lb shrimp, peeled and deveined
- 1 cup grits
- 4 cups water or broth
- ½ cup shredded cheddar cheese
- 2 tablespoons butter
- 1 tablespoon olive oil
- 2 cloves garlic, minced
- Salt and pepper to taste

Instructions

1. **Cook Grits:** In a saucepan, bring water or broth to a boil. Stir in grits, reduce heat, and simmer for about 20-25 minutes, stirring occasionally. Add cheese and butter, mixing until creamy.
2. **Preheat Grill:** Preheat your grill to medium-high heat.
3. **Marinate Shrimp:** Toss shrimp with olive oil, garlic, salt, and pepper.
4. **Grill Shrimp:** Grill shrimp for about 2-3 minutes per side until cooked through.
5. **Serve:** Spoon grits onto plates and top with grilled shrimp. Enjoy!

Sausage and Pepper Hoagies

Ingredients

- 4 Italian sausages
- 1 red bell pepper, sliced
- 1 yellow bell pepper, sliced
- 1 onion, sliced
- 4 hoagie rolls
- 2 tablespoons olive oil
- Salt and pepper to taste

Instructions

1. **Preheat Grill:** Preheat your grill to medium heat.
2. **Grill Sausages:** Grill sausages for about 10-12 minutes, turning occasionally, until cooked through.
3. **Sauté Peppers and Onions:** Toss peppers and onions with olive oil, salt, and pepper. Wrap in foil and grill for about 10 minutes until tender.
4. **Assemble Hoagies:** Place sausages in hoagie rolls and top with grilled peppers and onions.
5. **Serve:** Enjoy warm!

Grilled Chicken Fajitas

Ingredients

- 1 lb chicken breast, sliced
- 1 red bell pepper, sliced
- 1 green bell pepper, sliced
- 1 onion, sliced
- 2 tablespoons olive oil
- 2 tablespoons fajita seasoning
- 8 small flour tortillas

Instructions

1. **Preheat Grill:** Preheat your grill to medium-high heat.
2. **Marinate Chicken:** Toss chicken, peppers, and onion with olive oil and fajita seasoning.
3. **Grill Chicken and Vegetables:** Grill for about 10-12 minutes, turning occasionally, until chicken is cooked through and vegetables are tender.
4. **Warm Tortillas:** Warm tortillas on the grill for about 30 seconds per side.
5. **Serve:** Fill tortillas with chicken and veggies. Enjoy!

Corn and Avocado Salsa

Ingredients

- 2 cups corn (fresh or grilled)
- 1 avocado, diced
- 1 small red onion, diced
- 1 jalapeño, seeded and diced
- ¼ cup cilantro, chopped
- Juice of 1 lime
- Salt and pepper to taste

Instructions

1. **Combine Ingredients:** In a bowl, mix together corn, avocado, onion, jalapeño, cilantro, lime juice, salt, and pepper.
2. **Chill:** Let sit for 10 minutes to meld flavors.
3. **Serve:** Enjoy with tortilla chips or as a topping for grilled meats!

Grilled Apple Crisp

Ingredients

- 4 apples, cored and sliced
- 1 cup oats
- ½ cup brown sugar
- ½ cup flour
- 1 teaspoon cinnamon
- 4 tablespoons butter, melted

Instructions

1. **Preheat Grill:** Preheat your grill to medium heat.
2. **Prepare Topping:** In a bowl, combine oats, brown sugar, flour, cinnamon, and melted butter.
3. **Grill Apples:** Place apple slices in a grill-safe pan or foil pouch. Top with oat mixture.
4. **Cook:** Grill for about 15-20 minutes until apples are tender and topping is golden.
5. **Serve:** Enjoy warm with ice cream if desired!

Sesame Ginger Grilled Tofu

Ingredients

- 1 block firm tofu, pressed and sliced
- ¼ cup soy sauce
- 2 tablespoons sesame oil
- 1 tablespoon ginger, grated
- 2 tablespoons honey or agave syrup

Instructions

1. **Marinate Tofu:** In a bowl, whisk together soy sauce, sesame oil, ginger, and honey. Marinate tofu for at least 30 minutes.
2. **Preheat Grill:** Preheat your grill to medium heat.
3. **Grill Tofu:** Grill tofu slices for about 4-5 minutes per side until charred and heated through.
4. **Serve:** Enjoy with rice or in a salad!

Mango Salsa for Grilled Fish

Ingredients

- 1 ripe mango, diced
- 1 small red onion, diced
- 1 jalapeño, seeded and diced
- ¼ cup cilantro, chopped
- Juice of 1 lime
- Salt to taste

Instructions

1. **Combine Ingredients:** In a bowl, mix together mango, onion, jalapeño, cilantro, lime juice, and salt.
2. **Chill:** Let sit for 10 minutes to let flavors develop.
3. **Serve:** Enjoy as a topping for grilled fish!

Grilled Potatoes with Rosemary

Ingredients

- 1 lb baby potatoes, halved
- 3 tablespoons olive oil
- 2 tablespoons fresh rosemary, chopped
- Salt and pepper to taste

Instructions

1. **Preheat Grill:** Preheat your grill to medium heat.
2. **Prepare Potatoes:** Toss potatoes with olive oil, rosemary, salt, and pepper.
3. **Grill Potatoes:** Place potatoes in a grill basket or wrap in foil. Grill for about 20-25 minutes, turning occasionally, until tender.
4. **Serve:** Enjoy warm as a side dish!

Marinated Grilled Pork Chops

Ingredients

- 4 bone-in pork chops
- ¼ cup olive oil
- ¼ cup soy sauce
- 2 tablespoons honey
- 2 cloves garlic, minced
- 1 teaspoon dried thyme
- Salt and pepper to taste

Instructions

1. **Marinate Pork Chops:** In a bowl, whisk together olive oil, soy sauce, honey, garlic, thyme, salt, and pepper. Place pork chops in a resealable bag, pour marinade over, and refrigerate for at least 1 hour (or overnight for more flavor).
2. **Preheat Grill:** Preheat your grill to medium-high heat.
3. **Grill Pork Chops:** Remove pork chops from marinade and grill for about 6-7 minutes per side, or until cooked through and internal temperature reaches 145°F (63°C).
4. **Serve:** Let rest for a few minutes before serving. Enjoy!

Coconut Lime Grilled Chicken

Ingredients

- 4 chicken breasts
- ½ cup coconut milk
- 2 tablespoons lime juice
- 1 tablespoon lime zest
- 2 cloves garlic, minced
- Salt and pepper to taste

Instructions

1. **Marinate Chicken:** In a bowl, mix together coconut milk, lime juice, lime zest, garlic, salt, and pepper. Add chicken breasts and marinate for at least 30 minutes.
2. **Preheat Grill:** Preheat your grill to medium-high heat.
3. **Grill Chicken:** Remove chicken from marinade and grill for about 6-8 minutes per side, or until cooked through.
4. **Serve:** Enjoy with a squeeze of fresh lime!

Grilled Chocolate Banana Boats

Ingredients

- 4 ripe bananas
- ½ cup chocolate chips
- ½ cup mini marshmallows
- Aluminum foil

Instructions

1. **Prepare Bananas:** Slice bananas lengthwise, leaving the peel on. Gently open the banana to create a pocket.
2. **Fill Boats:** Stuff each banana with chocolate chips and marshmallows.
3. **Wrap in Foil:** Wrap each banana in aluminum foil.
4. **Preheat Grill:** Preheat your grill to medium heat.
5. **Grill Banana Boats:** Place foil-wrapped bananas on the grill and cook for about 5-10 minutes, until chocolate and marshmallows are melted.
6. **Serve:** Carefully unwrap and enjoy warm!

Taco Salad

Ingredients

- 1 lb ground beef or turkey
- 1 packet taco seasoning
- 1 head romaine lettuce, chopped
- 1 cup cherry tomatoes, halved
- 1 cup canned black beans, drained and rinsed
- 1 cup corn (canned or frozen)
- 1 cup shredded cheese (cheddar or Mexican blend)
- Tortilla chips for serving
- Optional toppings: salsa, sour cream, avocado

Instructions

1. **Cook Meat:** In a skillet, cook ground meat until browned. Drain excess fat and add taco seasoning according to package instructions.
2. **Prepare Salad:** In a large bowl, combine lettuce, tomatoes, black beans, corn, and cheese.
3. **Assemble:** Add the cooked meat to the salad and toss gently.
4. **Serve:** Serve with tortilla chips and optional toppings. Enjoy!

Chocolate Mug Cake

Ingredients

- 4 tablespoons all-purpose flour
- 4 tablespoons sugar
- 2 tablespoons unsweetened cocoa powder
- 1/8 teaspoon baking powder
- 3 tablespoons milk
- 2 tablespoons vegetable oil
- 1/4 teaspoon vanilla extract
- Optional: chocolate chips for added sweetness

Instructions

1. **Mix Dry Ingredients:** In a microwave-safe mug, combine flour, sugar, cocoa powder, and baking powder.
2. **Add Wet Ingredients:** Stir in milk, vegetable oil, and vanilla extract until smooth. Mix in chocolate chips if using.
3. **Microwave:** Microwave on high for about 1 minute and 30 seconds, or until the cake has risen and is set in the middle.
4. **Serve:** Let cool for a minute before enjoying directly from the mug!

Egg Salad Sandwiches

Ingredients

- 6 hard-boiled eggs, chopped
- 1/4 cup mayonnaise
- 1 teaspoon Dijon mustard
- 1 tablespoon chopped chives or green onions
- Salt and pepper to taste
- Bread for serving (white, whole grain, or your choice)

Instructions

1. **Mix Ingredients:** In a bowl, combine chopped eggs, mayonnaise, mustard, chives, salt, and pepper. Mix well.
2. **Assemble Sandwiches:** Spread egg salad on slices of bread, then top with another slice.
3. **Cut and Serve:** Cut sandwiches into quarters or halves and serve chilled.

Oven-Baked Fish Sticks

Ingredients

- 1 lb white fish fillets (cod, tilapia, etc.)
- 1 cup breadcrumbs
- 1/2 cup flour
- 2 eggs, beaten
- 1 teaspoon paprika
- Salt and pepper to taste
- Optional: lemon wedges for serving

Instructions

1. **Preheat Oven:** Preheat your oven to 425°F (220°C).
2. **Prepare Coating:** Set up three bowls: one with flour, one with beaten eggs, and one with breadcrumbs mixed with paprika, salt, and pepper.
3. **Coat Fish:** Dip each fish piece first in flour, then in the egg, and finally in the breadcrumb mixture, pressing to adhere.
4. **Bake:** Place on a baking sheet lined with parchment paper and bake for 15-20 minutes, or until golden and cooked through.
5. **Serve:** Serve with lemon wedges if desired. Enjoy!

Fruit and Yogurt Cups

Ingredients

- 2 cups yogurt (plain or flavored)
- 2 cups mixed fresh fruit (berries, banana, kiwi, etc.)
- 1/4 cup granola
  Instructions
1. **Layer Ingredients:** In cups or bowls, layer yogurt, mixed fruit, and granola.
2. **Repeat Layers:** Repeat layers until cups are filled.
3. **Serve:** Enjoy immediately as a refreshing snack or breakfast!

Zucchini Noodles

Ingredients

- 2 medium zucchinis
- 1 tablespoon olive oil
- 2 cloves garlic, minced
- Salt and pepper to taste
- Optional: grated Parmesan cheese for serving
  Instructions
1. **Spiralize Zucchini:** Use a spiralizer to create zucchini noodles (zoodles) or use a vegetable peeler for ribbons.
2. **Sauté:** In a skillet, heat olive oil over medium heat. Add garlic and sauté for 1 minute.
3. **Add Zoodles:** Add zucchini noodles to the skillet and sauté for 2-3 minutes until tender. Season with salt and pepper.
4. **Serve:** Serve warm, topped with grated Parmesan cheese if desired.

Homemade Salsa

Ingredients

- 4 ripe tomatoes, diced
- 1 small onion, diced
- 1 jalapeño, seeded and minced
- 1/4 cup cilantro, chopped
- Juice of 1 lime
- Salt to taste
  Instructions

1. **Combine Ingredients:** In a bowl, combine diced tomatoes, onion, jalapeño, cilantro, and lime juice.
2. **Season:** Add salt to taste and mix well.
3. **Serve:** Enjoy with tortilla chips or as a topping for tacos!

Pasta with Pesto

Ingredients

- 8 oz pasta (your choice)
- 1/2 cup pesto (store-bought or homemade)
- 1/4 cup grated Parmesan cheese
- Salt and pepper to taste
- Optional: cherry tomatoes or pine nuts for garnish
  Instructions
1. **Cook Pasta:** Cook pasta according to package instructions; drain and reserve some pasta water.
2. **Combine:** In a large bowl, toss hot pasta with pesto, adding a bit of reserved pasta water to help combine if necessary.
3. **Season:** Season with salt and pepper to taste.
4. **Serve:** Serve warm, garnished with grated Parmesan and optional toppings.

If you need more recipes or adjustments, just let me know!

4o mini

You said:

Mini Quiches Frozen Yogurt Bark

ChatGPT said:

ChatGPT

Here are the recipes for Mini Quiches and Frozen Yogurt Bark, formatted without line breaks:

Mini Quiches

Ingredients

- 6 large eggs
- 1 cup milk
- 1 cup shredded cheese (cheddar, mozzarella, or your choice)
- 1 cup chopped vegetables (spinach, bell peppers, onions, etc.)
- 1 cup cooked meat (ham, bacon, or sausage, optional)
- Salt and pepper to taste
- Optional: herbs for seasoning (thyme, oregano, etc.)

Instructions

1. **Preheat Oven:** Preheat your oven to 375°F (190°C).
2. **Whisk Eggs:** In a mixing bowl, whisk together eggs, milk, salt, and pepper until well combined.
3. **Prepare Muffin Tin:** Grease a muffin tin or line with muffin liners.
4. **Add Fillings:** Divide the chopped vegetables, meat, and cheese evenly among the muffin cups.
5. **Pour Egg Mixture:** Pour the egg mixture over the fillings, filling each cup about 3/4 full.
6. **Bake:** Bake for 20-25 minutes, or until the quiches are set and lightly golden on top.
7. **Cool and Serve:** Allow to cool slightly before removing from the tin. Serve warm or at room temperature!

Frozen Yogurt Bark

Ingredients

- 2 cups yogurt (Greek or regular, any flavor)
- 1/2 cup mixed berries (fresh or frozen)
- 1/4 cup granola or nuts (optional)
- 1 tablespoon honey or maple syrup (optional)

Instructions

1. **Prepare Baking Sheet:** Line a baking sheet with parchment paper.
2. **Spread Yogurt:** Pour the yogurt onto the prepared baking sheet and spread it into an even layer, about 1/4 inch thick.
3. **Add Toppings:** Sprinkle the mixed berries and granola (or nuts) evenly over the yogurt. Drizzle with honey or maple syrup if desired.
4. **Freeze:** Place the baking sheet in the freezer for at least 2-3 hours, or until the yogurt is completely frozen.
5. **Break into Pieces:** Once frozen, remove from the freezer and break the yogurt bark into pieces.

6. **Serve:** Enjoy immediately or store in an airtight container in the freezer for a refreshing snack!

www.ingramcontent.com/pod-product-compliance
Lightning Source LLC
LaVergne TN
LVHW081319060526
838201LV00055B/2368